LOVING PARENTING

Love Being A Parent

By
Linda Chatelain

ISBN: 978-1-938669-02-6
Linda Chatelain

Elisa, Antonio and Alex
  Thank you for being a part of my everyday life.
You keep me young and always looking for new things to learn.

LOVING PARENTING
  Thoughts On Parenting With Love
INTRODUCTION
LOVE ABOVE ALL
  Unconditional Love Defined
  Conditional Love Defined
LOVE YOURSELF
LOVE YOUR CHILD
LOVE BEING A PARENT
PARENTING WITH LOVE
  Build Loving Relationships
  Lovingly Allow Choices and Results
  Communicate with Love
  Recognize the Goals
    The 4 Goals of Negative Behavior
    The 4 Goals of Positive Behavior
  Love Changes- Be Flexible
IT IS UP TO YOU

INTRODUCTION

Over the past few years I have had been able to look at how I was as a parent when my children were growing up. I have often asked myself what I thought I did right and what I wish I could have done differently. Most parents don't get a second chance of trying again. Because of family circumstances I am blessed to have another chance to think about what worked for me as a single parent for so many years and what did not. As I raise three of my grandchildren, I am daily faced with new adventures in living as a family member with children I feel responsible for guiding and teaching.

As I have looked at my life as a single mother and now as a grandmother raising my daughter's children, one thing stands as truth. I love being a parent. It is a life calling I would not give up. The rewards are not only priceless but also so marvelous and wondrous they are almost indescribable. No other profession can offer as much variety or pleasure to me. It is with this belief I choose to share my thoughts with you. I want you to take a few minutes to stop and appreciate, even if it is only for a minute today, how wonderful it is to be a parent. I hope that one moment of love for the privilege of being a parent will extend to other areas of your life as well.

I am far from being an expert in the area of being a parent or a grandparent. I continue each day to do a little better than the day before. These ideas and thoughts are just a few of the things that have been of help to me. These ideas and thoughts are a very small sample of the many things I have learned over the years. They are only a place to begin and build upon. Perhaps one of the thoughts is something you have already pondered but haven't tried yet. So here is a reminder to follow your instincts and be a parent full of love.

LOVE ABOVE ALL

Love is the very center of effective parenting. Love makes the difference between someone who just cares for a child and being a caring successful parent. The focus of love is a determining factor between acting as a caring parent and falling into a pattern of abuse or neglect. With love a parent will think about their child's best interest. When love is misdirected a parent can find they think about personal needs without concern about the effects on others. Being an effective loving parent requires a commitment to the child, a desire to make a difference in their life as they grow and develop.

There are two kinds of love that exist in life. The first is unconditional love. The second is a conditional love based on actions, feelings and results. While unconditional love is the ideal, conditional love is far superior to a lack of any love. Everyone needs to feel that they are loved in some way, by someone who is important to them and who cares about positive outcomes.

Unconditional Love Defined

The first principle of parenting is love. At the very center of being a parent is unconditional love. Unconditional love is the deepest kind of love that you can give. It is the purest form of love to either give or receive.

Unconditional love is just as it implies, love without conditions. It is love without requirements or expectations of any kind. There are no expectations of love being given in return. Unconditional love is given freely, without thought. Unconditional love doesn't wait to be asked for. It leaves the heart without regard to whether it is wanted, asked for, waited for or expected. Unconditional love doesn't vary based on personal perceptions of the person it is given to. It doesn't grow or wane from day to day based on changing views. It is not affected by judgment of any kind. It doesn't ask for opinions before it is given. It is not based on views of good or bad. Unconditional love is not changed by behavior of the person it is given away to. Unconditional love is being able to separate the person from the acts they choose and loving the person anyway.

Unconditional love is given from the heart. It does not and is not a part of the physical world of material means and matter. It exists whether one gives something physical or not. Loving someone unconditionally does not mean giving them anything. It is a feeling, a presence of mind that is positive in their behalf and, at times, a prayer in your heart for them. It is possible to love someone unconditionally and not give them any money or physical show of support. Unconditional love can be given from a distance. Because it is based on thought and spirit it can exist and travel with ease from the giver to the receiver without word, action or acknowledgement.

Unconditional love grows as it is given away. A small spark of love escapes the mind and grows into a feeling that feels the heart. That feeling is something so strong that it cannot be kept inside and is simply given to the universe as a gift to be bestowed on the recipient. The giver doesn't have to do anything except acknowledge the love and allow it to be. The recipient may never know from where the love comes, but is simply filled with a feeling of worth and warmth.

Unconditional love is the miracle that heals the heart. Unconditional love cannot exist in the presence of negative feelings of hurt, anger, victimization or fear. Unconditional love is so powerful an emotion that it overcomes all other feelings. It is so pure and bright that it outshines and enlightens everything it comes in contact with. Unconditional love brings the giver an enlightenment of their own life, feelings, understanding of truth and a peace in knowing the truth and release of emotions that have been tied up in the feelings of the relationship.

Unconditional love builds self-worth in all involved. The giver has a sense of worth knowing they can love, regardless of actions or feeling of another. He can govern or choose for himself. The receiver has self-esteem knowing he is capable and worthy of being loved even without being perfect. He is lovable simply be of who he is.

Conditional Love Defined

Conditional love is just as it implies, based on one or more conditions the giver feels are necessary, required or present before the expression or act of love is extended. Conditional means the level of love may vary. Conditional love is often given freely as unconditional love is withdrawn later when the giver does not feel it returned by a certain date or with an expected level of emotion. Conditional love is frequently identified when a person/parent can only love to the extent they are loved in return. Conditional love asks the receiver to value the desires of the giver over themselves. Conditional love destroys or undermines person worth rather than builds on self-esteem. When love is used as a measure of worth or acceptance, conditions on love imply if someone isn't loved as expected, they are less of a person of worth than others they see receiving the love they desire.

Conditional love is often present in abusive or controlling relationships. The control factor is love given or withdrawn. The controller begins "I will love you if...." The ending may vary but the meaning is clear each time. If the person obeys or acts as told they will be or are worthy of love and/or respect. If they choose not to obey/act as directed they do not get love or respect. This love is used to shift the guilt and blame. The person withholding the love, though controlling or abusive, feels vindicated and free, claiming or accusing that harming as opposed to loving is acceptable or necessary. They rationalize their behavior by claiming they would give the love, and are capable of loving, but the person, by not meeting the conditions set forth, does not want their love. So the often decide, whether consciously or not, that if they cannot contribute love to the relationship they will give the opposite, which is usually negative attention.

Conditional love rarely, if ever, fosters good relationships. Conditional love denies compromise, ignores free emotion and destroys initiative. Conditional love does not invite honest communication or cooperation. Conditional love pushes people away rather than welcomes.

LOVE YOURSELF

Loving parenthood begins with the ability to love yourself. Too often when you become a parent the new child becomes your center of attention, your focus in life. You end up losing your own personality and interests in the process of parenting. You may set aside your interests and dreams in order to be what you think a good parent is.

Love yourself unconditionally. It is necessary to love yourself unconditionally before you can love others unconditionally. You cannot give away what you do not have. If you do not have the skills and ability to love yourself unconditionally, you cannot have the skills to love someone else unconditionally. If you have not experienced unconditional love from self or from others, you do not know what you can give away. Unconditional love for self means looking past flaws, mistakes, lack of skills or perceived lack of wisdom. Love yourself with passion in spite of how you believe, think or act. Love you just because you are who you are.

Step back and reclaim yourself. Remember what you wanted to be and what was important to you before that first child arrived to share your time and be a part of your life. Put that dream back up on the refrigerator where you can see it. Instead of dreaming about someday, share your dreams with your children. Doing so will not only make you feel more worthwhile but will teach your child the importance of looking for something that is different, something new or exciting. Allowing yourself to believe in a dream, even a readjusted one, will give you and your child the power of belief in yourself, each other and life itself. Shake off the talents you decided you didn't have time for and use them in new ways as a parent. Grab a good book to read and go to the park with your toddler. He will love being able to play on the slides and swings while you read that novel you put away. Read the classics, those books you enjoyed as a child and promised yourself you would read again someday. Let today be a waited for day of adventure and escape. Feel the excitement of those you love as they discover your old friends with a young heart and the imagination of youth.

Let go of perfection. Allow yourself be less than perfect in the way you are, the ways you act, the ways you think. Being perfect is nearly impossible, especially all the time. Seeking perfection involves time that as a parent you probably do not have an excess of .Let perfection be something that other people stress over becoming. Use the stress energy you save to take an extra walk around the block alone, to play a game of catch with your son or to bake a batch of cookies for a Saturday afternoon tea party in the garden. Stop trying to be the perfect parent or the "good" parent you read about in the manuals and in classrooms. Begin being your child's best parent. There is no perfect parent. There are many theories for parents to look at and think about. How can you expect to be the best parent when even the authorities, the psychologists and clinicians do not agree on what perfect is? You cannot be perfect if there is no perfect standard to match yourself to. So stop striving for perfection. Be the best of what you can be with the knowledge you have. Learn something new today so tomorrow you are able to choose from even more bits of wisdom. Be the best you at this moment. Let go of who you were yesterday, of who you are not. Don't look for who you might be tomorrow or stress over what may not be. Simply be the best you already are today.

Love the person you see in the mirror. You are your own best friend. No one knows you better than you know yourself. Others may see the persona you portray or the masks you wear, but you are the one alone who knows everything about you, both good and bad. You may seek approval from others, but the opinion that really counts is the one you have of your own self. Learn to accept the person you have become through the experiences that life has allowed you to participate in. Practice unconditional love with yourself. You are a person, neither good nor bad, and deserve your own love simply because you are. Love unconditionally the person in the mirror that has flaws as well as perfections. Love the mixture that you are. Love the color of your skin, the feelings you have and the culture you embrace as who you are. Separate yourself from the actions you choose. Look at the things you choose to do and decide if you want to continue but in the meantime love yourself unconditionally If you feel you are not worthy of love because of choices you have made, then now is the perfect time to love yourself. Love yourself for believing there are choices you may make which will make as much of a difference to your future as your previous choices made in your past.

Seek loving relationships. Experience the touch of another person in your life, whether it is physically or emotionally. Love yourself enough to allow a friendship to develop with someone you know. As you experience love from outside you can recognize more of what is already within. Love yourself enough to accept love from others with an open mind and an open heart. As you experience the flow of love from others, you will learn how easy it is to give love in little ways, unexpected ways and perhaps previously unthought-of ways.

Love yourself enough to stand up for you. There is no one better able to say "I am important too!" When others lash out at you in anger, love yourself enough to step back and take a deep breath. Perhaps the anger will not sit so heavily on your heart. Love yourself enough to learn to stand a little firmer so that you are prepared for the next barrage your child may throw at you in his quest to find his way. Love yourself enough to say, "This is enough." Love yourself enough to admit that what you have been doing is not working and be willing to make a change. Love yourself enough to make a change in your own best interest even if your child does not agree with you. If the choices of yesterday are not working for today, then love and believe you can choose something better, something different or something new.

LOVE YOUR CHILD

Love your child. It doesn't matter whether your child is a boy or a girl, love him for being your child. It doesn't matter whether your child was planned for or not, he/she is here now and is a part of you in this moment. It doesn't matter whether your child is one you physically were a part of creating or someone created you were given to care for or chose to care for. It doesn't matter when, where or how they came into your life. They are a part of that life at this time, so love them for just being here for the present moment.

Love your child for the unique individual that he/she is. Be thankful t there is only one person exactly like him. Love what is unique about him and embrace that part as given to you as a gift to enjoy. No other parent will learn the lessons you will learn from this particular child or have the same experiences. Love your child for the smile that drives you crazy because even if his words are saying I'm sorry his face isn't. Love him for the way he has of tilting his head and looking away when he wants you to believe he is telling the truth but can't look you in the eye because he knows you will see right through him. Love your child for the disability he has that assists you in being a different person than you ever dreamed you would be.

Love your child for the teacher he is. No other parent will learn the lessons you will learn from this particular child or have the same experiences as you will. Children are teachers in everything they do. Love them for it. Love your child for teaching patience because she wants to show you that she can tie her own shoe. Love your child for teaching you the wonder of nature as he brings you a baby worm or a slow moving snail to watch. Love your child for the lessons she teaches you in looking for the beauty of nature around you when she brings you a bouquet of dandelion flowers to keep forever and ever. Love your child for taking the time to teach you about hope and belief as he scans every blade of grass knowing he will find a four-leaf clover to give you for luck. Love your child for teaching you life is to be enjoyed and there is always something new to see, explore or learn about. Love your child for the lessons he teaches you in the importance of honest, effective communication. Love him for teaching you not everyone hears the same message from the same words. Love your child for teaching you that anger brings rebellion while love brings cooperation.

Love your child for allowing you to develop the teacher and leader within yourself. Love him for allowing you to walk ahead of him so he can follow in your footsteps. Love him for his belief in you that you are wise and already know all the answers to all the questions of the universe. Love your child for the trust she gives that you will love her no matter what she does. Love your child for letting you teach him one more lesson, to share one more joke, or to pass on the traditions and knowledge of someone you learned from. Love your child for asking you to show him how to be just like you. Love your child for letting you teach him right from wrong and expecting you to walk the same way you talk, for holding you to a higher standard than you may otherwise hold yourself. Example speaks louder than word, so live what you want him to learn. Love her for asking you to be her teacher as she tries out life on a day to day basis but is afraid to do it alone.

Love your child for the opportunity of watching life unfold in a different way. Love him because he has not had to learn the same lessons in the same way as you did. Love him for the opportunity he gives you of watching how another life, another person, develops as he faces the everyday happenings of life. Love your child for the innocence she has in approaching each new life challenge with excitement and joy. Love your child for being in your space to show you that life is always about choices and results and different choices bring different results.

Love your child for the trust he has in you that if he falls you will be there to pick him up, brush off the dirt and help him back on, encouraging him to try again. Love your child for the faith if something goes wrong you will be there to make everything all better for her. Love your child for his trust that you will provide everything he needs or could ever need so he is free to just live life his way and do the things he enjoys. Love your child for his trust you will love him no matter what he does, who he is or where or goes, why he makes a choice or how he chooses to learn. Love her for the belief that even if she tells you she hates you one day and wishes you were dead or threatens you she still expects you will do whatever it takes to bail her out of jail the next day.

Love the beautiful person you know is lost beneath all the anger, frustration and revenge when you do not go along with her wishes. You saw her beauty, energy, friendliness, trust and hope when she was younger. It is the knowledge of good within which sustains your love even when you yourself are in deep pain and anguish because of the present rift in the relationship that may take years to heal along with all the patience and understanding you can gather. Love the little boy beneath the adult façade that still wants to live life his own way while playing at being adult in a world expecting him to be grownup and responsible.

LOVE BEING A PARENT

Love being a parent. It is the most wonderful thing you can be in this life. There is no other life opportunity that will bring you so much joy or so much sorrow. No other life experience requires of you as much as the calling of being a parent. Where else in life do you have to be so spontaneous, willing to risk and open while still providing stability and security? Being a parent is all that anyone has ever described and even more things there are not adequate words for.

Love the job of being a parent. It is the most rewarding exciting occupation you can have. There is never a dull moment. It is more exciting than any amusement park ride you can think of. It is the most challenging role you will ever encounter. Parenting will require all the knowledge you have and require you to continue learning each and every day. Parenting affords you the chance to be both a teacher and a student at the same time.

Love the experience of never knowing what will happen next. Love the experience of being trusted one moment and doubted the next. Love the experience of feeling a finger tightly grasped by a small hand clinging for safety and in what seems like only moments, a hand pulling to get away to explore life on his own. Love the experience of going from diapers to coveralls to jeans to tuxedos because your child grows up before you can stop to take a breath. Love the experience of worrying one day about your daughter taking her first unsteady steps, crying the next as she skips down the road on her first day of school, worrying again as she is whisked from your grasp to her prom and a mix of worry and sorrow as she walks down the aisle to her future. Love the experience of looking into the eyes of a day old angel one day, the hurt eyes of a fallen toddler the next, the wounded eyes of a friendless youth, the confused eyes of a struggling teenager until you finally see love returned by a new parent who suddenly understands himself the price you paid.

Love the small special moments of being a parent. Love that middle of the night time no one knows about except you when the only sound in the house was the personal lullaby you sang with a choked up voice and tears in your eyes. Love the time you got to admit you were not perfect and you apologized to your child. In that moment you taught him no one is perfect, everyone makes mistakes and needs to say I am sorry once in a while. Love the moments you sat up all night holding a fevered child because he could only sleep in your arms. Love the moment when you find out that the child the school teacher knows is not anything like the one you thought you were sending to school each day. Love the moment after you disciplined your child harshly and he turned around with tears in his eyes and said "I know you love me anyway." Love the moment when you thought you could not hang on one moment longer and your daughter brought you her favorite bunny to sleep with so you would have good dreams. Love the moment when your son said he didn't want to live there anymore so you put up the tent in the backyard to keep him warm in case he didn't really want to run away. Love the moment when while fishing from the bank of a river you listen as your five year old son explains where babies come from. Love the moment when your children climb on your lap, put their arms out as far as they can and say "I love you this much." Love the moment, for it may only happen once, when your child says "You were right, I shouldn't have..." Love the moment when your teenager faces off and says "I wish I were never born" and you reply, "I thank God every day you were." Love the moment when your baby holds her own baby.

Love being the proud parent. Love watching your baby walk across the stage to receiver her diploma and feel the relief in your heart you both made it through. Love sharing with others the off-tune soloist singing his heart is part of your family. Love the feeling of warmth filling your heart when your son receives the Eagle Scout Award he thought he wouldn't earn. Love claiming the ballerina who stole the show from her adoring audience. Love being the one in the crowd that the speaker seeks out to introduce to the crowd as his mother or father. Love being able to cheer from the stands for the basketball player you always wanted to be without embarrassing him in front of his friends. Love being the parent your child's friends ask to drive them to early-morning class every day because they know they can be themselves around you. Love being able to clap until your hands hurt for the marching band flutist that everyone knows can't walk very far without being in major pain but refuses to let her classmates or teacher down. Love being the one waiting at the finish line for the winner as she crosses the finish line.

Love looking for the joys of being a parent in unusual places and times. After pacing the hall with a colicky baby at 2 a.m. love the moment when he lays his head on your shoulder and surrenders to your love. When the kids are running rampant through the house and the youngest hides behind you and yells safe, look for the tiny moment where he considers you a protection from harm and feel the joy, if only for a second before you are both tackled by the racing bodies behind him. When you want to spank the child who just hasn't listened all day, look first at the joy in knowing he has learned to stand up for his own feelings and desires in his own way, and love being his parent. When you are working to wash the lipstick off the wall for the 10th time this week take a moment and look for the joy in having such a creative, imaginative little girl who wants to make your house "so beautiful".

Build Loving Relationships

Parenting with love involves being able to form long lasting loving relationships. A loving relationship does not just magically appear. It involves blending love, understanding, patience, forgiveness, trust and a whole lot of faith. There are four basic ingredients that assist in the development of positive relationships. They are mutual respect, taking time for fun, encouragement and communication.

Respect is defined as "reverence and admiration toward a person, place or thing." Respect is "a feeling of reverence and admiration given for reputation, work or attributes." Mutual respect would be a feeling of reverence and admiration given for each other based on reputation, work or attributes. Respect is something that is generally earned in some way because of something someone has done, for which they stand for or are an example of. Respect can be shown through many ways. Words conveying a feeling of love, reverence, gratitude, trust and faith are some of the most common ways of expressing respect. Actions of obedience, kindness, patience, understanding, following an example and love send messages of respect from one to another. Even such simple things as a hug, a smile, a wave or the touch of a hand can tell someone there is admiration in place. Ironically it is the respect we give to someone else that earns us the respect we would like to receive in return.

Mutually respecting one another involves looking for the good in the other person and recognizing it in some way. Mutual implies the agreement and cooperation of at least two people. It means looking past the obvious flaws and respecting the person anyway. Mutual respect can only be given and received with love.

The most loving way to teach cooperation is to provide opportunities to work together. Make a conscious choice to make the relationship the most important part of the chances you create. Make the value of the relationship the reason for working together and not what will be accomplished. How the dishes are stacked or the bed is made on a particular day is of little importance. The information you share about and with each other while you wash the dishes or sweep the floor is invaluable. A small wrinkle on the bed of today is minor compared to the value of a child who knows for many tomorrows he is a valuable member of the family.

Grow positive relationships between children and parents by having fun together. Fun is simply enjoying being together in a pleasurable activity that makes you smile, laugh or, sometimes, just relax and forget your cares and worries. Fun doesn't have to cost much. You can share a wide possibility of activities with little or no money at all. Share a joke or funny story. Go on an excursion to the zoo. Have a picnic at the local park. Take a nature walk in the canyons. Create an obstacle course in the backyard and have a day of races and simple competitions. While the sprinklers are on run through the water together, play tug of war or have a water fight. Go to the local thrift store and purchase books to read together or games (board and card) to play.

Make a date for love. Many articles on keeping a marriage alive talk about the importance of scheduling time together as husband and wife. Couples get caught up in the business of everyday routine and give away their time to activities instead of relationships. The same is true of family members we care about. Too often we get caught up in the routines of homework, chores and household maintenance or community activities to spend time alone with those we love. So schedule small love dates with your child. Take him to a movie and a dinner, just the two of you. Go window-shopping for a new dress and go to lunch, just the two of you in a fancy restaurant. Go for a stroll around the neighborhood and learn about her best friend. Pick up a child and go play in the sand at the park while she tells you all about her new favorite toy.

Build loving relationships through encouragement. Build self-esteem with blocks of love. The base of self-esteem is belief. Encourage your child to believe in himself. Encourage him in trying new skills and let him know how well he does with each new one he attempts. Encourage her to expand on her talents. Let her know the things you see she has a talent for and help her to develop it through practice. When you recognize something of value give your child the tools he needs. If she is an artist, buy her paints and brushes and pencils to experiment with. If your child is excited about finding the answers to everything find him things to explore and study. Buy a cheap radio at a garage sale that he can take apart and put back together in order to understand and learn about electronics, schematics, blueprints and order. If your little dancer can't take lessons right now because of financial reasons, purchase an old dance record she can dance to whenever she wants and practice the steps she has already learned. Encourage her to make up her own dances and put on a show just for you or the family. Have a young singer in your home? Record some songs off the radio he can practice singing along with.   Build self-esteem by pushing a little harder for his best performance, his best try and accept each try with a smile. What is more important for a child's self-esteem, being able to get straight A's if he honestly is struggling with a subject or being able to look you in the eye and say, "I did my best"? Expect their best, accept their best and honor the best in them.

Build loving relationships through communications. Talk to each other in love and with love.   Share your feelings about the other person. Communicate what you like about them. Communicate what you would like to feel from them. Tell your child how you feel about being a parent. Share your hopes and dreams with your child so he knows it is okay to dream and look toward a new day with excitement. Talk with your child about how you wish you didn't have to work. Explain to your child how you feel about going to work each day so you can provide for the family yet sometimes you wish you could be home with her instead. Communicate with each other the lessons you learn and the lessons you would like your children to learn. Explain why you do not agree or approve of a behavior or choice instead of just telling him it was wrong. Communicate what you find of value in the show you watch together. Why did you choose it, what would you change about the show and why? Communicate you are sorry for the harsh word, the discipline you had to choose in order to teach the lesson or the mistake you made in understanding how they felt. Communicate it is all right to be wrong, try again, ask for forgiveness or let the other person be right too. Communicate love, respect, feelings and anything your mind and heart want the other person to know so you can grow and stay close.

Lovingly Allow Choices and Results

Lovingly allow your child to experience the result and consequences of his choices. Love her enough to let her hurt because of her choices. Love him enough to let him learn from the lessons he chooses the same way you learn from the lessons and opportunities present in your own life. Your child is no better or worse than you. Love him enough to believe if you can withstand all that happens in your life, including the results you experience because of their choices, he too is capable of handling, in a unique way whatever shows up for him to overcome.

Love your child enough to remember everyone does not choose the same and allow him to choose in his own way as long as it does not hurt you or someone else you are responsible for. Set boundaries with love and allow him to make a number of choices within those limits. Love him enough to set rules and standards and clearly state the consequences of non-agreement and non-conformity. As you set the rules, boundaries and standards, allow your child to feel your love and concern along with loving trust they can make wise choices if they desire; then lovingly step aside and let him create the results.

Allow the consequences to follow. Natural consequences are those which permit a child to learn from the natural order of the physical world, such as hunger comes from not eating. Logical consequences are those which permit a child to learn from the reality of the social order, such as if he can't obey the rules, he can't play. In setting consequences with your child, follow the basic principles. Understand the child's goals, behavior and emotions. Be both firm and kind. Don't try to be a "Good" parent, it doesn't exist. Become more consistent in your actions. Separate the deed from the doer. Encourage independence while controlling safety. Avoid pity, remembering that choice has brought them to this point. Refuse to be over-concerned with what other people will think. Recognize who owns the problem and allow him to carry the burden. Refuse to fight or give in to pressure or emotions. Let all the children share the responsibility when appropriate. If the children have been told not to eat in the bedroom and mother finds dishes left out, let all the children experience the consequence. Pointing a finger to only one encourages tattling and blame. Allow them to all learn together and to work together to follow rules.

Lovingly allow him to stand alone if that is how he needs to learn. The results he creates may be exactly right for him but not exactly what he expects. You can stand with love in the background watching or ready to assist or offer advice. When he is old enough, honor his choice to not be a part of your life if his choices in friends or lifestyle pull him a different direction. Trust if he is old enough to choose his friends and supporters he is old enough to deal with the results of those friendships and the decisions they make together. Love him enough to not get in the way of the results even if they are not pleasant for him to experience.

Allow her to love others as much as you love her. Allow her to make the choice not to receive your love for a time if she desires. Let her seek love elsewhere in order to feel a different love, seek happiness or prove something if necessary. Your support may not be what she thinks she wants or needs at the moment because she is not willing or able to receive that particular love in the present moment as she struggles to find her way or be independent. Your love will not be any less for her if she is not standing by your side. Your love is safe in your heart whether she allows you to show that love right now or not. Continue to love her silently and unconditionally.

Communicate with Love

Communication is the art of both listening and being heard. When I say it is an art, I am not exaggerating. Some people have a natural talent for communicating everything effectively, clearly and powerfully so no one misunderstands their meaning. Most of the rest of society develop skills that work well for us if we use them and promote many misunderstandings when we forget. Communicating effectively with love involves not just talking, telling what you think, feel or want, but also being able to listen for more than just the words from the other side of the partnership. Communication is a partnership. Communication is the sending of a message from one source to another and the receiving of a message or information by one source from another. A speaker generally needs a listener or communication does not exist. You can't be a good listener if there is no one or nothing of value to listen to.

Effective communication involves many things. It involves having purposeful conversations that help you understand the other person or what the other person is sharing. It involves reflective listening; listening for the message and then reflecting back to the sender what it is you thought you heard and how you perceived it. It involves "I" messages, which are basically blame free messages about your positive feelings, and things that bother you. It is important to have a nonjudgmental attitude that respects the other person. Use appropriate timing. An apology will not usually be heard in the heat of a battle. The listener will not hear the message of love and concern if the conversation is in front of their friends or they feel embarrassed. Avoiding pressure, sarcasm and ridicule keeps the conversation open and honest. This often goes along with the advice not to use labeling and generalities. Make sure if you talk with a person you talk about the situation at hand not a general opinion that may or not have a bearing on reality in this instance. Show your faith and confidence in the other person through your words, gestures and tone of voice.

Communicate with the music of love. When you go into a store or a shopping mall what is the first thing you usually hear? In most major stores there is some kind of music playing. The music playing automatically communicates whether that store wants you to shop leisurely or act quickly without thought. If you have ever gone shopping with your children think about how the stores vary in the choice of their music. A large department store catering to adults will play soft rock or mellow melodies appealing to a person's desire for comfort, peace, leisure or desires. Go into a toy store and the music playing is nursery rhymes, songs from children's movies or learned in school. No wonder when your child goes in he wants to buy everything and so do you. What is the music in a clothing shop catering to youthful fashion? It is upbeat and rock, fast and rhythmic. It appeals to a teen's desire to be part of their peer group; it reminds them they are not their parents and encourages them to be different, to be a little wild. It invites the kids in to choose alone while most parents wait outside. Just as music appeals to our senses and is a tool of communication, so is the tone of our voice when we communicate. When you tell your child you love her does your voice convey love, peace or harmony? When you encourage your child to try something new do your words say you agree but the tone of your voice infer you are not so sure this is good for him or what he should be trying? Is it possible to say I love you and convey anger and resentment? Sure I have done it lots of times. The words get lost in the music of the voice and what is heard and felt is the disgust beneath.   Communicate what you really want the other person to hear by matching the words with the tone of your voice, the rhythm of your voice and the speed that the words are spoken.   Make up your own song of love. Love singing your song. Once you find your personal song, love the opportunity to sing it daily. Loud and clear sing "I Love Parenting."

Develop the love skill of using "I" messages.   Express your feelings, explain what you feel, communicate a need or a desire without accusing, demanding or demeaning the other person. "I" messages take off the burdens and allow the feelings to be expressed more clearly. "I feel", "I see", "I wish" and "I like" are powerful. "I" messages are specific. "I" messages often include such phrases as when or if. "I" messages explain the feelings or desires by including the phrase because and then clarifies the reasons. There is a big difference in what is communicated between saying "I feel sad when I do not think you listen to what I say because I want you to learn" and saying "You never listen to me. You'll never learn."   There is an invitation to love and choose different if you say, "I feel sad when I think you are too busy to play because I like being with you." There is a demand for attention and accusation if you state "You are always too busy to play with me." If you want the other person to feel guilty or bad the second phrase would certainly be a good tool, but it would not convey love or understanding. Practice "I" messages with yourself and then with your children.   Use these phrases regularly. These phrases hold within them approval and acceptance. They convey there is a second person with their own feelings and leave the conversation open.   "I like the way you made your bed this morning" establishes a greater feeling of respect than simply saying, "Great, you made your bed." Using "I" messages leaves the conversation open for the other person to also use "I" messages, encouraging sharing of feelings and honest, open communication of how to better build a closer relationship.

Listen better than you speak. Listen more than you speak. Listen with love. When you listen, expect and listen for the good, the love, the feelings, and the desires not only in the words but in the tone of the voice, the facial expressions and the body language. Surprise yourself and listen not only with your ears but with your heart. The words may reach your ears but the feelings will reach your heart and mind. Care about what your child shares with you. If it is important enough for them to share it is important enough for you to listen to.

Listen with an open mind. Take off and discard the filters that block what you hear or how you hear what someone says. Listen without judgment based on your own experiences and beliefs. Everyone has not had the same chances to experience life in your way, so be open to a different viewpoint and don't decide what you hear before you hear it. Remember when listening to your child you have had many more experiences than he so his ideas really may be less cloaked in feelings left behind from previous lessons. Understand each experience has either made you a better listener or it has not.

Listen to understand. Make sure what you hear is what was said. Listen and then give feedback. Reflect back the feeling you felt, the expression you saw or the words you thought you heard. Clarify that you were listening to what they meant to say. Listen once, ask, and then listen again. You will be surprised at how much more you hear the second time.

Recognize the Goals

Behavior, whether good or bad, positive or negative is a perceived idea unique to each parent. What some parents see as misbehavior or negative behavior is seen by another parent as simply a child's way of pushing his limits. There is no such thing as misbehavior. A child simply behaves. It is the perception of the behavior that determines whether it is seen as either positive or negative. There are some behaviors that society in general sees as less-than acceptable while other behaviors society encourages as something to be developed with enthusiasm.

The 4 Goals of Negative Behavior

Most negative behavior fills one of four goals for a child. . These are: Attention, Power, Revenge or A Show of Inadequacy. To understand which of the goals is at the center of the negative behavior, take a look at your own reaction and feelings as a parent. Are you feeling guilt, anger, frustration, uneasiness? What is your first reaction to the negative behavior? Are you ready to give in, do you take a power stance yourself or do you run from the fight? Once you have identified the behavior choose your reaction carefully. To change the behaviors you dislike, change your reactions. React in a new way, a different way and an unexpected way or don't react at all to negative behavior. Act toward positive behavior and stop reacting predictably to the negative you do not like or want to continue.

Attention is one of the most common reasons for perceived negative behavior. A child, especially a young child, wants to know you are near, accessible and care about him. He craves your attention and either consciously or unconsciously attempts to gain your attention in some inappropriate manner. I have heard many mothers complain that it seems their young ones seem to choose when mom is the busiest to misbehave. This observation is not far from the truth when you stop and honestly look at what is happening. If you are busy fixing dinner and a child wants to tell you about something exciting they found, mother will often brush them away with "Talk to me later. I am too busy." In a young child's mind later is an unknown time period. Often later is only a minute away in their fast paced world. So later is when they try to get your attention again by pulling on your apron strings or playing at your feet or asking a different question you may think is important enough to stop and listen for a minute. Even a good child strives to get attention. Recognizing effort before they need to ask for it helps head off one form of this need. If you son has been working hard at keeping his room clean but you haven't noted it, he may go in his room to play with a toy and then leave it out. Mom sees this as negative behavior and reacts by telling him to clean up his room. She tells him he has been doing well and she is disappointed in seeing it so messy now. Success. All he really wanted in the first place was to know mom liked it and knew he was keeping his room clean. The price of mom being temporarily disappointed was worth the complement he had been looking for and missing. Lovingly find ways to give your child your regular attention. Note the little things he does each day. Give him attention for doing the small things, whether expected of him or not. Give him a hug as he walks out the door and let him know you noticed he brushed his hair and teeth without being asked. Give him attention without his having to ask for it. Pop your head around the door to just say "Hi." If you are thinking about him while you are folding his pants you just washed, let him know it. Pay attention and listen intently when he speaks and he will not have to find as many other ways to get attention. Pay attention to the color of the barrettes your daughter wore to school. As you tuck her into bed share how much you liked that color of barrette in her hair. She will feel good about herself and be assured you pay attention to her even when she isn't looking or asking. Catch your daughter in a good moment and give her positive attention and you will soon find she asks for less negative attention by doing something unusual for her. Catch your son playing quietly and acknowledge the moment and you may find he learns that crashing trucks are not the only way to get your attention.

Negative behavior is often nothing more than a struggle for power. It could be a need to feel a child has power over himself, someone else or even you the parent. . When a child feels out of control they naturally seek control by seeking to gain some sort of power. Exerting his power is often a way of seeking independence or growth. Think of the child standing there with his hand on his hips, looking just like you, saying, "you can't make me". When a child is behaving negatively in order to assert his power or his need to control his environment or the opportunity to choose for himself, take a look at your own feelings and reactions. When a child engages you in a power struggle what is your common reaction? React differently. Could you allow him to be right or powerful? Can you use this moment to teach him compromise and how to create win-win solutions? Use this time to take a look at your own power beliefs about your relationship. Is it time to let go of control in an area where he needs to grow? Is it time to allow more choices and a sharing of reasons for your decisions? Maybe you can give up control in one area and refocus on control in another area where your child needs direction and guidance. Allowing your child to be right, to exert some control and make his own responsible choices in the major areas of his life will allow him to be able to give up struggling so much in the areas of less importance. Working out who can be in charge in certain situations allows your child to learn that even when he doesn't agree life brings experiences where it is safe to let others be the ones in charge. Instead of having a daily power struggle over what time he will go to bed, give him a chance to choose his bedtime from two times you are comfortable with. Be flexible and bendable and power becomes less of a struggle. If it is important to remain firm, then allow him to be make choices of how it works. If bedtime is at 9:00 then don't fight over the time. Be firm on the time but let him chose whether he would like to have a talk or a bedtime story as part of the bedtime routine. Create opportunities for him to exercise power appropriately under your direction and within the boundaries of his environment.

A child who is stuck in anger or feels overly controlled will often revert to negative behavior in the form of revengeful words or actions. Revenge is identified by a desire by the child to hurt, lash out or get back at someone. Revenge is an effort to hurt back for a perceived hurt experienced   Revenge is also a game that a parent and child can play. Each takes turns hurting the other. It is a higher level of power struggle. Communicating with love your understanding of how the child feels helps to calm the feeling. When a child wants to use revenge to show his feelings take the time to talk with him and find out what he is feeling. He may not understand what he is feeling and may be seeking revenge because he needs someone to blame for not feeling better. What does he think the negative behavior will accomplish for him? What does he want or need to prove to himself or someone else? As a parent look at your own feelings. How do you respond to the child who wants to get revenge? Do you respond with a similar attitude or with love and understanding? Do you give in to his demands to keep the peace, teaching him that this is indeed a good way to get what he wants from you and society? A child who uses revenge as a tool is generally looking for loving guidance and support in learning more appropriate forms of dealing with hurt, anger and pain. Unconditional love is invaluable in letting them know that while their behavior is not acceptable they still are.

The fourth negative behavior commonly used by children to achieve their goals is a show of inadequacy or a call for help. Even though the child is capable of performing a task he acts as though he cannot. When a parent's desire is to overprotect or to save a child from having to perform, this behavior is often at play. This is the child who knows the answers to the problems but waits for mother or father to come to help him. This child waits until the night before the project is due to ask his parents for help because he is sure if he says he can't do it in time, mom or dad will stay up all night with him to get it completed or better yet will finish it for the child while he sleeps. A loving parent can recognize this behavior as a cry for help and attention. Instead of lovingly assisting the child, a parent may step back and let the child find a workable solution for himself. The wise loving parent will lift, edify and cheer from the sidelines allowing the child to complete the task using his best skills, talents and knowledge. This way the child grows from the experience.

The 4 Goals of Positive Behavior

The challenge comes to parents to lovingly discourage negative behavior. So what behavior can we with love encourage them in learning and making a part of their life. One suggestion is to look for the four goals of positive behavior and develop their use. The 4 goals of positive behavior are: I belong by contributing, I can decide to be responsible for my own behavior, I am interested in cooperating and I can decide to withdraw from conflict.

Encourage a child to contribute to the family and to society. There is no place else that affords a better environment for contributing than in the home. Provide opportunities to serve others, to reach out to others, to be an example. A child wants to feel like he contributes to the world he is in. He starts by contributing to being a part of his family. Starting with helping mother with little chores and then going on to do nice acts of service and love for brothers and sisters, a child learns he is valuable to others and has something to give to make the world a better place as a result of his efforts. The more a child contributes within the family circle the more he will be able to develop sight into where he can contribute in his school, his circle of friends and his community at large as he grows.

A child wants to be responsible for his own actions. Being responsible involves taking the consequences and experiencing the results he creates. A parent can lovingly assist a child to learn and develop responsibility for his actions and decisions by providing boundaries and limits that are understandable and reasonable. Ask your child what he thinks are reasonable expectations. You may be surprised at the answers you receive. Sometimes the ideas and expectations they have for themselves are even higher than ones you may have considered. As a child is learning sometimes tools such as time outs, loss of privileges, extra chores or compensation can mimic   more serious adult consequences such as time in jail, community service and fines. Take the time to talk with your child about what he thinks responsibility means and how you can assist him in learning to be more responsible. Encourage him to draw up a contract with you. Include how and what he expects you to teach. Include in the contract what he will learn and how he accomplish the goal. For both parties include the consequences of breaking the contract and the expected results if the contract is fulfilled. Assist your child in being responsible. If a child steals or shoplifts a pack of gum you taking it back doesn't teach responsibility, but allowing the child to admit the mistake, and face those he has wronged gives him a pride in being honest and responsible, in making conscious positive choices. Realize a child pushing for more independence is asking to be given more responsibility for his life. Show him all the love you can as you help him find his own way of taking on his future in a positive way.

A child has an innate desire to cooperate and to work with others. They love to feel like they are helping mother or dad. This is the beginning of service to others. Parents teach cooperation by giving the child loving opportunities to be a part of making decisions that affect others as well as him. Playing games together, building and creating projects around the house all teach cooperation and working as a team. The skills of cooperation allow a child to work in occupations where each member counts yet all work together toward a common goal or objective. Helping dad fix the sink by handing him the tools teaches a child there are different ways to cooperate.   Cooperation is developed by effectively sharing toys, belongings and even sharing a room. Sharing a room with a younger sibling requires the older child to learn how cooperation develops in different stages and it is okay to change, to compromise, to give in and sometimes others will do the same. Siblings learn how and when to give each time alone yet learn to work together to maintain a pleasing environment for both. Cooperation is learning there is no right or wrong, only different perceptions and both perceptions can be right. Solutions involve working together for the best outcome for both. Teaching a child to cooperate requires love and patience. Set the example by showing love when making compromises, creating win-win solutions and helping each other in your roles as mother and father. Cooperation by example means dad is willing to help mom with her household duties and mother returns the efforts by making sure dad has help with his responsibilities. The biggest, most loving way to teach cooperation is by example. Let your child see you working together with your partner and they will learn to look for opportunities to cooperate not only with you but with others.

The fourth goal of good behavior is to develop the knowledge and skills to enable a child to choose when to withdraw from conflict. Nothing strengthens this skill more than teaching about love with love. Teach a child to respect and love himself as a valuable person who does not have to prove his worth at every turn. Along with love, teach your child positive ways to recognize and express his feelings. Conflicts generally arise over differences in feelings and opinions. Teach your child to respect the opinions of others and accept there are many ways of looking at situations, people, places and things. When he is secure in the knowledge differences are opportunities to learn, he will not feel a need to defend his stand or enter into conflicts. Teach your child patience and tolerance by example. How you deal with conflict and upsets is what he will learn. Teach him how to work out differences before they become conflicts by treating him as you want him to be. Being able to withdraw from conflict might involve overcoming a tendency to bully or control others through violence and abuse. Teach him to develop his strengths and have confidence in himself that he can choose positive solutions or overcome obstacles he thinks he sees. Remember every problem does not have to be solved by him or by you. Some problems and situations will evolve on their own without any intervention. Part of this goal is learning to not choose to go into battle over every belief or idea that comes along. Lessons in how to withdraw from conflict may involve learning to do his best and not be so competitive. It is okay to let someone else win the race and be the one to cheer someone on, knowing the best efforts of each are what count.

Love Changes- Be Flexible

No parenting idea or technique is going to work every time or even with every child. Each time you enter a new teaching situation, it is a new experience. What worked last time may not work this time or it might. What worked for one child may not work with another child because of personality differences and relationship differences. Be open to inspiration as to which method will work best in each particular instance. Have faith you can choose appropriately as long as you stay centered in and deal from love. One thing is true, when it comes to being a parent there is no exact right or wrong way to be. There are as many ways of being a parent as there are parents. The most important part of being a parent is to be the best one you can be for each individual child. Love the role you play with each one. Love the variety each child develops in you.

Love the opportunity to keep learning. Keeping one step ahead of your child will keep you young in heart and mind. Look around at how other parents treat their children and learn. Attend parenting classes offered at local schools or churches to learn something you didn't know before or get a fresh perspective on your relationship with a child. Read articles and books on how others have grown through or survived the joys and sorrows of being a parent. Join a support group and share ideas and insights. Meet with other parents and learn that your child is no different than any other. Learn new ways of showing love on a daily basis that will touch your child in the way that he learns best. Learn and identify the languages of love (Service, Touch, Appreciation, Time and Gifts) your child prefers. What is the best way to touch his heart and mind? Learn how to speak his language fluently and then speak it often. Receive the gifts of love as freely as you give them. Let your children know the way you like to have love shown, then watch for them to present their gifts of love in small, humble ways.

Love the flexibility of life. Teach your child that life is unpredictable and fun. Life doesn't have to be a certain way, allow it to happen occasionally without effort. Focus on the present moment, forget about yesterday and don't worry about tomorrow. Just let tomorrow come as it will. When something arrives in your life to experience, don't worry about how it happened; focus instead on what you can do now or where you go from here. Go with the flow of life and energy. You can't control it all. Sometimes you have to just let life flow on, either with you, around you or past you.

Embrace with love a changing you. You can never change the other person. The only person you can change is you. Don't waste your time and energy in looking for ways to change those you love. Look at yourself and decide the areas of your life and personal traits or beliefs you want to change. Look at yourself and ask what or how you want to love more. In choosing lasting changes, make changes you want to make for you not for someone else. Choosing for you is choosing life and you deserve to have the life you are willing to work for and even love the life you choose. As you change others will have the opportunity to both change and move with you or remain the same and move away from you. Choose to use the moments of your life in new ways. Use the moments to teach, love, praise, play hug and be with those you love like you have never done before. Search in the small moments for the joy, the lesson, the sunshine, the chance or the feeling it holds just for you. Become an inspiration to others in becoming their best, trying something new or learning to grow. Become a creator in life. Create life around you through beauty, music, art, song, dance, thought, word or deed. Change your smile and share it, pass it on. A smile is contagious; it cannot stay with only one person.

It is up to you to decide what you do with these thoughts and ideas. What I have thought about and what has worked for me is done. I have shared with you enough to get your own mind working. Now it is up to you to choose something you haven't tried before. Now it is up to you to find something new that works and maybe share it with me. Whatever you do, make sure it is your best.

Take a few minutes this evening, after you have tucked your children into bed, to reflect on the joys and sorrows being a parent bring you. Don't worry about whether someone else would think they were a joy or a sorrow. What others think is of no importance in this moment. The important thought is the one that comes to you right now. Do you love being a parent? If not, why not? If you do, what are the things that make you grateful? I challenge you to take one of the joys you find and post it on your wall to look at each day or put it in your wallet where you will see it regularly. Keep the joys and the reasons in mind and enjoy the journey of life with your family.

Now go stand in the doorway of your children's rooms. As you look at each child ask yourself the question, "What do I love about being this child's parent?" Let the answer come easily to you, for it will. Allow yourself to be surrounded by the silent love that bonds you together, whether you want it to or not. Feel the warmth of love inside of knowing not only do you love them, but they love you for the unique person you are and the influence you have in their life. Keep the love circulating between you like the water in a spraying fountain, giving life to everyone it touches. Through love spread the message of how you keep Loving Parenting.

Contact:
Linda Chatelain
West Jordan, UT
lchat1950@hotmail.com

Version 2
Published September 2013

www.ingramcontent.com/pod-product-compliance
Lightning Source LLC
Chambersburg PA
CBHW060634030426
42337CB00018B/3361